Am I in It?

by Mickey Daronco and Diane Ohanesian

I can see Kit go in it.
Can Kit fit in it?

Kit can sit in it.

Pam can sit in it.

I see Sam go in it.
Sam can fit in it.

Can I go in it?
Can I fit in it?

Is the fat cat in it?
Is Pat in it?

Is Sam in it?

Is Vin in it?

I am in it!